A NOTE TO PARENTS

Reading Aloud with Your Child

Research shows that reading books aloud is the single most valuable support parents can provide in helping children learn to read.

- Be a ham! The more enthusiasm you display, the more your child will enjoy the book.
- Run your finger underneath the words as you read to signal that the print carries the story.
- Leave time for examining the illustrations more closely; encourage your child to find things in the pictures.
- Invite your youngster to join in whenever there's a repeated phrase in the text.
- Link up events in the book with similar events in your child's life.
- If your child asks a question, stop and answer it. The book can be a means to learning more about your child's thoughts.

Listening to Your Child Read Aloud

The support of your attention and praise is absolutely crucial to your child's continuing efforts to learn to read.

- If your child is learning to read and asks for a word, give it immediately so that the meaning of the story is not interrupted. DO NOT ask your child to sound out the word.
- On the other hand, if your child initiates the act of sounding out, don't intervene.
- If your child is reading along and makes what is called a miscue, listen for the sense of the miscue. If the word "road" is substituted for the word "street," for instance, no meaning is lost. Don't stop the reading for a correction.
- If the miscue makes no sense (for example, "horse" for "house"), ask your child to reread the sentence because you're not sure you understand what's just been read.
- Above all else, enjoy your child's growing command of print and make sure you give lots of praise. *You are your child's first teacher—and the most important one. Praise from you is critical for further risk-taking and learning.*

—Priscilla Lynch
Ph.D., New York University
Educational Consultant

To Chris
—L.J.H.

To John
—J.W.

Text Copyright © 1994 by Lorraine Hopping Egan.
Illustrations Copyright © 1994 by Jody Wheeler.
All rights reserved. Published by Scholastic Inc.
CARTWHEEL BOOKS is a registered trademark of Scholastic Inc.
HELLO READER! is a registered trademark of Scholastic Inc.

Library of Congress Cataloging-in-Publication Data

Hopping, Lorraine Jean.
  Wild weather. Tornadoes! / by Lorraine Jean Hopping : illustrated by Jody Wheeler.
    p.   cm. — (Hello reader! Level 4)
  Summary: Describes the work of two people who study tornadoes in the Midwest by discovering and following them.
  ISBN 0-590-46338-1
  1. Tornadoes—Middle West—Juvenile literature. [1. Tornadoes.]
I. Wheeler, Jody, ill. II. Title. III. Title: Tornadoes!
IV. Series.
QC955.H76 1993
551.55'3—dc20   92-27947
                                                 CIP
                                                  AC

20 19   0 1 2/0

Printed in the U.S.A.   23

First Scholastic printing, March 1994

⚡ WILD WEATHER ⚡

Tornadoes!

by Lorraine Jean Hopping
Illustrated by Jody Wheeler

Hello Reader!—Level 4

SCHOLASTIC INC.

New York   Toronto   London   Auckland   Sydney

Chapter 1

In the Path of a Tornado!

The air was hot, sticky, and still.
A good sign.
Dark thunderclouds crackled
over the road ahead.
Even better.

Scientist Tim Marshall
and his friend Roy Britt
knew they were close.
But they weren't sure how close.

Then it happened.
A spinning funnel of wind
dropped from the sky.
Less than a mile away,
it smacked the ground. Hard.
The giant funnel was white
and almost noiseless.
It kicked up clouds
of dust, branches, and
bits of unknown objects.

That's it! Tim thought.
It was what he had hoped for—
a tornado!

Tim and Roy are tornado chasers.
They film and study tornadoes.
Tim and Roy must drive very close
to the deadly storms.
On that spring day,
they almost came too close.

Tim parked the van
southeast of the tornado.
That's usually the safest spot
for filming.
The reason is that
tornadoes normally travel
from the southwest
to the northeast.

Then the two tornado chasers
set up their tools:
video cameras, tripods, and a TV
for watching weather reports.
Tim and Roy watched the tornado
twist across the Texas plain.
They felt safe.
The tornado was moving away
from them.
They filmed the action.

Then the tornado changed direction.
It made a big, choppy circle.
It was heading toward Tim and Roy!
The tornado was now chasing them,
instead of the other way around!

Tim and Roy quickly tossed
everything into the van.
They jumped in and sped away.

Tornadoes usually travel about
30 to 50 miles per hour.
That is under the highway speed
limit.
But some tornadoes go 70 miles
per hour.
That's way too fast to outrun—
even in a van!
If the tornado did catch Tim and Roy,
the winds could pick up the van
and throw it like a deadly missile.

To avoid the tornado, Tim and Roy
had to drive into a hailstorm.
Chunks of ice as big as softballs
cracked the windshield.
The van rocked and rolled
in 60-mile-per-hour winds.
But the deadly tornado
missed them.

It crossed the road
just behind them.
It ripped some trees
right out of the ground.
Then the funnel lifted up
and out of sight
in a wall of rain.

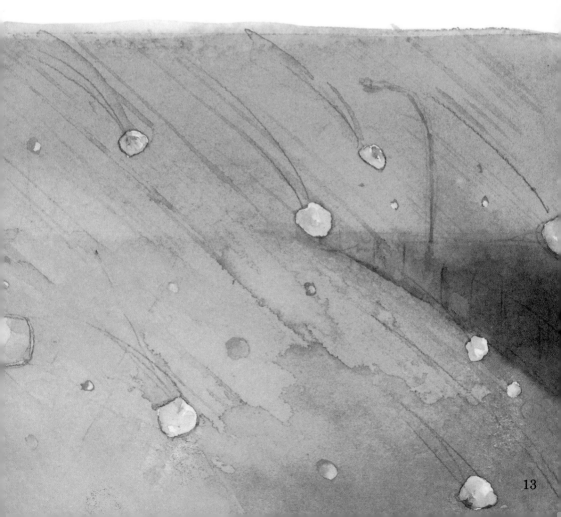

Chapter 2

Spinning Funnels

Tornadoes are the most powerful
storms on Earth, for their size.
These mighty storms are
tall, skinny funnels
of spinning air.
The funnels stretch from the ground
to mountain high clouds—
about 15,000 to 20,000 feet!

Their winds are among
the fastest on Earth.
They can blow up to
300 miles per hour,
which is almost as fast as
a DC-10 jet.

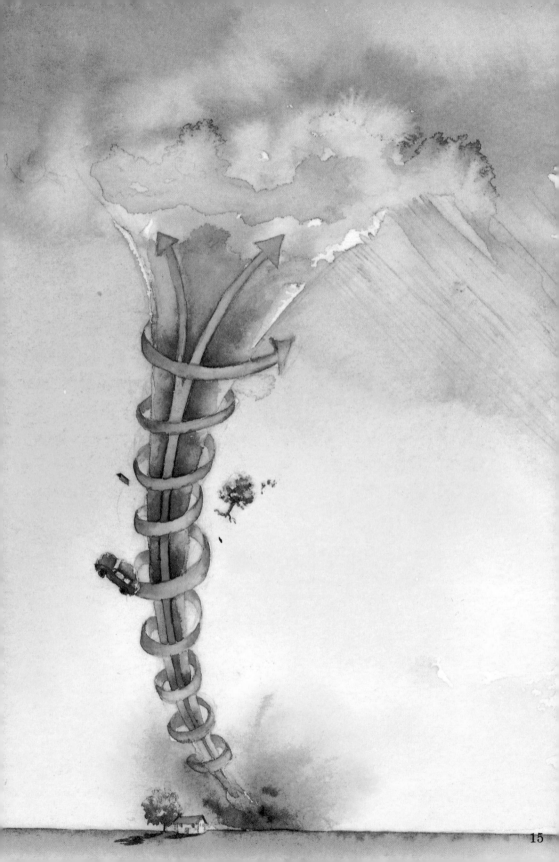

The world's fastest winds can cause some of the world's worst damage.

~ 1890 ~

In 1890, a tornado in Massachusetts blew away roofs and walls of houses. But the furniture inside was just fine!

In 1928, a tornado in Kansas plucked the feathers right off some chickens!

In 1931, a tornado in Missouri
lifted an 83-ton train . . .
and tossed it 80 feet off the track!

– 1931 –

In 1948, a tornado in Iowa
flipped a house upside down.
But the house stayed together!

· 1991 ·

In 1991, a tornado in Missouri
tore up a patch of lawn—
the grass and roots!
It left behind only smooth mud!

The United States gets more
tornadoes than any other country—
an average of 800 tornadoes every
year.
Each year, dozens of Americans die
from these tornadoes.

TOTAL TORNADOES
(CONTINENTAL U.S.)
STATE AVERAGES (1962 – 1991)

ALABAMA • 22	NEBRASKA • 37
ARIZONA • 4	NEVADA • 1
ARKANSAS • 20	NEW HAMPSHIRE • 2
CALIFORNIA • 5	NEW JERSEY • 3
COLORADO • 26	NEW MEXICO • 9
CONNECTICUT • 1	NEW YORK • 6
DELAWARE • 1	NORTH CAROLINA • 15
FLORIDA • 53	NORTH DAKOTA • 21
GEORGIA • 21	OHIO • 15
IDAHO • 3	OKLAHOMA • 47
ILLINOIS • 27	OREGON • 1
INDIANA • 20	PENNSYLVANIA • 10
IOWA • 36	RHODE ISLAND • 0*
KANSAS • 40	SOUTH CAROLINA • 10
KENTUCKY • 10	SOUTH DAKOTA • 29
LOUISIANA • 28	TENNESSEE • 12
MAINE • 2	TEXAS • 139
MARYLAND • 3	UTAH • 2
MASSACHUSETTS • 3	VERMONT • 1
MICHIGAN • 19	VIRGINIA • 6
MINNESOTA • 20	WASHINGTON • 2
MISSISSIPPI • 26	WEST VIRGINIA • 2
MISSOURI • 26	WISCONSIN • 21
MONTANA • 6	WYOMING • 12

U.S. TOTAL: 825 TORNADOES

*less than one

Tornado chasers study tornadoes
close up.
That way, they can tell when and
where the next tornado may form.
This helps weather experts
warn people to take cover.

Some chasers, like Tim and Roy,
work by themselves.
Others are part of a team of experts
at the National Severe Storms
Laboratory (NSSL)
in Norman, Oklahoma.
The lab is in the heart of
Tornado Alley.
This is an area, from Texas
to the Dakotas,
where more than half of all U.S.
tornadoes touch down.

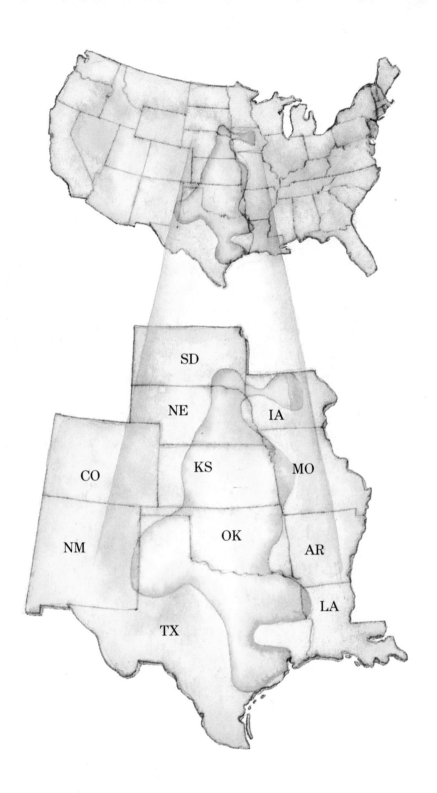

Each spring,
hundreds of tornado chasers
go to Tornado Alley.
Most tornadoes take place
in April, May, and June.
Texas, Oklahoma, and Kansas
are the hardest hit states.
But a tornado could form
in any month, in any state.

Chapter 3

The Chase Begins

Tornado chasers don't wait
for a tornado to hit
and then go try and find it.
The tornado would be long gone.
Most only last minutes or even seconds.

Also, tornadoes may be tall,
but they're usually skinny.
Some can be very skinny.
A tornado might wreck one house
and never even touch
the house next door!

They are so fast and skinny that
Tim Marshall catches a tornado
only one out of every 10 chases!

It takes lots of planning
to find a tornado.
Most tornadoes form
in the afternoon.
But Tim goes to work
early in the morning.
He needs time to study the weather.
He has to map out a chase route.
And he has to get there.
He may drive hundreds of miles
from his Texas home
during a single chase!

First Tim calls the National
Severe Storms Forecast Center.
He asks for information
about the weather.

Tornadoes form inside
huge thunderstorms.
These storms can span
several states.

Tim wants to know
if any storms are in the area.
So he checks with the radar experts
at the Storm Center.

Radar tracks thunderstorms
as they move.
The storms show up on a
radar screen as blobs of color.

The chasers hope one of those blobs
has a hook pattern,
like an S or a 6.
That stands for a funnel cloud—
and funnel clouds can
become tornadoes!

The most likely spot for a tornado
is along a storm front.
That's where a large mass of cold air
meets a large mass of warm air.

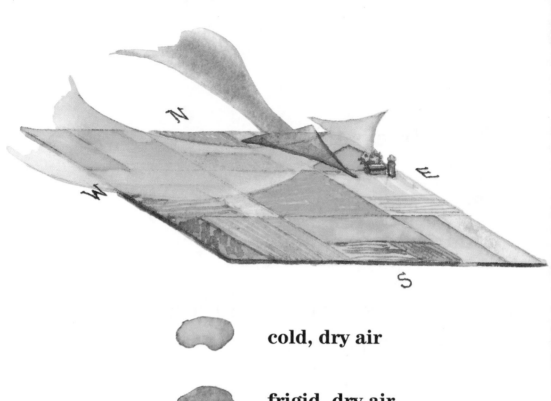

cold, dry air

frigid, dry air

warm, wet air

This is how a funnel cloud forms
in Tornado Alley.
Cold, dry air blows in from the west.
It sits high in the air.
Colder, higher air may blow in
from the north.

Meanwhile, warm, wet air blows in
from the south.
This air is low to the ground.

Normally, warm air rises.
But when a double blanket
of cold air
sits on warm air,
the warm air can't rise.
The cold air is blocking it.

And the cold air can't drop,
as it normally does.
The warm air is in the way.

So the masses of air slide, twirl,
and push against each other.
They make crazy-shaped clouds
and strong winds.

Finally, some warm air may punch
a hole up into the cold air.
It looks like a giant
mushroom cloud.
This rising warm, wet air cools.
Rain or hail begins to fall.
Then the cloud may start to spin,
like water going down a drain.
This spinning cloud is called
a funnel cloud.

On the radar screen
at the Storm Center,
the funnel cloud looks hook-shaped.
The Storm Center sends out
a tornado watch.
This is a message that tells everyone
in the watch area to take cover
in case a tornado touches down.

Everyone, that is,
except the tornado chasers.
They get into their cars,
vans, jeeps, and trucks.
And they drive off to meet
the brewing funnel head-on!

They watch and film the funnel cloud.
As the winds get faster,
the cloud spins
in tighter and tighter circles.

About half the time,
a funnel cloud breaks up
and disappears.
But at other times,
a funnel cloud drops
down from the sky
and touches the ground.
Touching down turns a funnel cloud
into a tornado.
Some people in Tornado Alley
call it a twister.

Chapter 4

It's a Twister!

Every tornado, or twister,
has its own color, sound,
and shape.
And each twister
behaves differently.

Usually, a tornado's color
matches the color
of the ground.
Reddish dirt makes
a red tornado.
Some tornadoes are white.
Others may be gray or
brown.

Tornadoes can sound like
a hundred jets taking off . . .
or a thousand roaring trains . . .
or a million buzzing bees!
But some tornadoes,
like the ones on the open plains,
make very little noise.

The sounds are caused
by objects that
the tornadoes hit
or pick up and carry.

A tornado's shape may be
its strangest feature.
People describe tornadoes
in many different ways.
Someone said one tornado
looked like the trunk
of a giant elephant.
It sucked up water, dirt, trees—
everything in its path.

Then it rose into the sky
and disappeared.
People have said that
tornadoes have looked
like barbershop poles, hourglasses,
wobbly spinning tops,
slithering snakes,
and even a giant lawnmower!
This twister "mowed" down
a strip of trees in a forest.

Tornadoes also do different
kinds of damage.
A weak tornado might blow off
the roof of a house
but leave the walls standing.

A strong tornado can splinter
a house to pieces.
Only a bathroom or
inside closet
may be left standing.

Super strong tornadoes
can send pieces
of wood sailing through the air,
only to land like porcupine quills
in a mattress!

Chapter 5

Life-Saving Scientists

If a tornado can wreck a house,
imagine what it can do
to a tornado chaser!
Luckily, so far, no chasers have been
directly hit by a tornado.
Many, though, have come close.

Tornado chasing has
other dangers, too.
One danger is lightning.
Lightning occurs in all thunderstorms.
The electric bolts usually hit
the tallest object in an area.

On the open plain,
the tallest object is often a human.
In 1983, lightning struck
right next to five tornado chasers.
Luckily, they all lived.

Car accidents are another danger.
Tornado chasers have also been hurt
in car crashes.
Sometimes, they were driving and
sky-watching at the same time.
Other times, they got hit by cars
that were fleeing the same storm
they were chasing.

Hail is a danger, too.
The falling chunks of ice
can hit hard enough
to break windows
and dent cars.

"Usually, if we stay in the car,
the car gets pounded,
but we don't," said Tim.

So why do these scientists
risk their lives?
They do it to save the lives
of others.
The number of tornado-related
deaths has dropped
in recent years.
One reason is that tornado chasers
have helped the Storm Center
warn people faster.

"Tornadoes are hard to predict,"
said Tim. "They're dangerous.
But they're very, very exciting."

TORNADO TIPS

- Never, ever chase a tornado!
Leave this very dangerous job
to the experts.

- In a tornado, stay inside a building.
It is safer to be on the lowest floor—
a basement or cellar, if there is one.

- Go to a bathroom or a closet
that is in the middle of the building.
Close the door. Cover yourself with
something big, like a mattress.

- If you're outside, go inside.
If you can't, lay face down
in the lowest spot you can find.
Cover your head with your hands.

- If you're in a car or a mobile home,
get out. You are better off in a solid
building or a ditch.